Introduction

Prior Knowledge

Children must have the following skills before they are ready to do the practice activities in these shopping mall centers:

- identify and know the value of bills and coins
- how to "count-on" using money
- counting by 5, 10, and 25
- adding and subtracting amounts of money
- serial addition
- using calculators to check answers
- telling time

Using Center Activities

Although the activities in this book are organized in order based on increasing difficulty, any center can require only that children figure total cost and make change. Centers requiring children to calculate taxes, discounts, etc., can be used at your discretion. Each activity needs to be taught and demonstrated before having the students do it on their own. See page 12 for an explanation of this process.

In addition, children will need to know:
- how to get out and set up the materials
- procedures for doing the activity
- procedures for handling problems that arise
- acceptable noise level and movement about the room
- teacher's attention signal and student responses
- how to organize and put away the materials

Setting Up Centers

The directions for each individual store contain signs and forms needed in the center. There is also a list of the types of items you might include for "sale."

Set up your centers so that there is a traffic pattern leading the buyers past the information and the items for sale on "shopper's" way to the clerk's table.

Post signs, lay out merchandise to sell on one table, and place all items need-ed to run the center on another table.

Each store in your "shopping mall" will be set up in a similar manner and contain certain items in common.

In preparing for the centers, items to sell will need to be collected. These can be items from around the classroom, items sent from home (see letter on inside back cover), or items from thrift shops and yard sales.

The items will need to be labeled individually or, if there are only a few types of items being sold, you may have a sign showing the prices. You can use stick-on dots containing prices or make a set of tags to tie onto the items for sale. With the exception of a few consumable items, children return items to the store when they have finished their task or at the end of each center time.

- wall space for posting signs
- tables for displaying merchandise
- a "cash box" with play money
- a name tag or button for the manager/clerk
- a place to return "purchases" at the end of center time
- a tax table where needed
- a purchase or receipt form
- pencils
- calculator

Math at the Mall

Shoppers and Clerks

In every center, the shopper and clerk will follow these general steps.
Specific directions for certain stores will be described on their individual direction pages.

The Shopper will:

- go to the bank and get the appropriate wallet and task card.
- go to the "store" and select items to buy.
- figure out the cost to see if they have enough money.
- hand the items to the clerk and pay the amount.
- count any change to see that it is the correct amount.
- return to his/her desk to do the task card job.
- return items purchased to the store.
- return the wallet to the bank.

The Clerk will:

- put his/her name sign below the store name.
- check to see if the cash box contains the amount listed on the lid.
- add up the cost of items for each customer.
- fill in the receipt form.
- take payment and make change.
- put the purchased items in the shopping bag.
- put the items from the "return" box back on the table.
- take the extra money from the cash box and return it to the bank.
- take down his/her name sign.

Getting Started

Brainstorm

Ask children "What is a mall?" Once you have a description put up a "Yes - No" chart and have children come up and write their names in the column to answer the question "Have you ever bought anything at a mall?"

Finally make a list of all of the shops and businesses they can name that can be found in a mall. Use the list to create a "Store Directory" by putting the list in alphabetical order. When the list has been completed, ask children "Which stores have you been to?"
Make a tally mark by each store as it is named.

Finish by having children count up the responses for each store and graph the results.

A Mall

grocery

department store

shoe store

flower shop

Bank

Explain that this bank will be used as a place to pick up "wallets" containing the money and the task cards they will need for buying things in the classroom mall. They will go to the bank at the beginning of each center time to pick up their wallets and return them at the end of the period.

Stores

Make a general introduction to the classroom mall. Children will be "walked through" the centers in great detail before they actually do them. This is just an overview.

Identify each store by name and point out where it is located in the room. Explain what will be sold at each one. Use one store for modeling the process that shoppers and clerks will follow.

Shopping Bags and Name Signs

Guide children through the steps to make their own shopping bags to use when they are shoppers and name signs to use when they are clerks. Directions for these are found on page 10.

Reproduce and use as a sign for this store in your classroom mall.

Our Class Bank

Put paper clip through here.

—

Today's Banker

You will need to have wallets containing play money for children to spend. Old wallets and purses would be fun to use, but you would need quite a few if your whole class was shopping at the same time. The following directions use large, sturdy envelopes and the form on page 7 to create wallets in which to put the money and the task cards that the children use in the centers. You will need to make several for each center. Three or four students could be shopping at a store during center time.

Determine in advance how much money children will need for a given center. In some cases, a center calls for children to pay in only bills or only coins. The "wallets" should contain only that type of money.

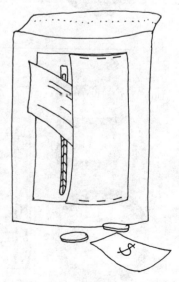

Place the money in the envelope and slip a task card appropriate to the center in each wallet.

In the beginning, the teacher or an aide may need to be in charge of the bank depending on the level of your students. The job of "banker" is to pass out the correct wallets to the shoppers at the beginning of center time. At the end of center time, the banker collects any "profits" from the stores and refills each wallet.

Note: Reproduce this form to use with the directions on page 6 as you make wallets for your "shoppers."

1. Cut out the pattern.
2. Fold on the line.
3. Staple the sides.
4. Glue the wallet to an envelope.

Store: _____   **My Wallet**

This wallet contains: _____

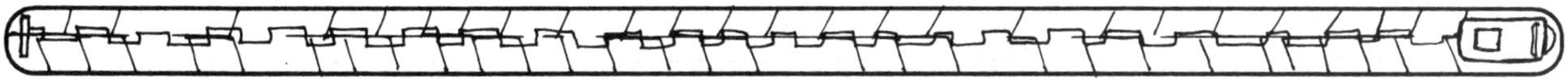

fold up

Reproduce these forms to use at any center where you want children to have the experience of recording purchases and costs.

Please Pay Clerk

Item	Price

Date: _____ **Total** | |

Please Pay Clerk

Item	Price

Date: _____ **Total** | |

Please Pay Clerk

Item	Price

Date: _____ **Subtotal** | |
Tax | |
Total | |

Please Pay Clerk

Item	Price

Date: _____ **Subtotal** | |
Tax | |
Total | |

Note: Reproduce this form for centers requiring a tax table.

$ $ $ $ Tax Table $ $ $ $

If the total is:	Tax:						
.01 - .25	.01	4.51 - 4.75	.37	9.26 - 9.50	.75	14.01 - 14.25	1.13
.26 - .50	.03	4.76 - 5.00	.39	9.51 - 9.75	.77	14.26 - 14.50	1.15
.51 - .75	.05	5.01 - 5.25	.41	9.76 - 10.00	.79	14.51 - 14.75	1.17
.76 -1.00	.07	5.26 - 5.50	.43	10.01 - 10.25	.81	14.76 - 15.00	1.19
1.01 -1.25	.09	5.51 - 5.75	.45	10.26 - 10.50	.83	15.01 - 15.25	1.21
1.26 - 1.50	.11	5.76 - 6.00	.47	10.51 - 10.75	.85	15.26 - 15.50	1.23
1.51 - 1.75	.13	6.01 - 6.25	.49	10.76 - 11.00	.87	15.51 - 15.75	1.25
1.76 - 2.00	.15	6.26 - 6.50	.51	11.01 - 11.25	.89	15.76 - 16.00	1.27
2.01 - 2.25	.17	6.51 - 6.75	.53	11.26 - 11.50	.91	16.01 - 16.25	1.29
2.26 - 2.50	.19	6.76 - 7.00	.55	11.51 - 11.75	.93	16.26 - 16.50	1.31
2.51 - 2.75	.21	7.01 - 7.25	.57	11.76 - 12.00	.95	16.51 - 16.75	1.33
2.76 - 3.00	.23	7.26 - 7.50	.59	12.01 - 12.25	.97	16.76 - 17.00	1.35
3.01 - 3.25	.25	7.51 - 7.75	.61	12.26 - 12.50	.99	17.01 - 17.25	1.37
3.26 - 3.50	.27	7.76 - 8.00	.63	12.51 - 12.75	1.01	17.26 - 17.50	1.39
3.51 - 3.75	.29	8.01 - 8.25	.65	12.76 - 13.00	1.03	17.51 - 17.75	1.41
3.76 - 4.00	.31	8.26 - 8.50	.67	13.01 - 13.25	1.05	17.76 - 18.00	1.43
4.01 - 4.25	.33	8.51 - 8.75	.69	13.26 - 13.50	1.07	18.01 - 18.25	1.45
4.26 - 4.50	.35	8.76 - 9.00	.71	13.51 - 13.75	1.09	18.26 - 18.50	1.47
		9.01 - 9.25	.73	13.76 - 14.00	1.11	18.51 - 18.75	1.49

Personal Shopping Bags

These bags serve two functions. They offer a place for children to transport goods within the center and to their desks. They also provide a place to keep track of which centers children have been to and whether they were the shopper or clerk.

Materials:
- copies of the form on page 11
- brown paper shopping bags (with handles if possible)
- glue

Steps:
1. Children color in the form and cut it out.

2. They glue the form to the shopping bag.

3. Students fill in their *Shopping Record* form at the end of the center time.

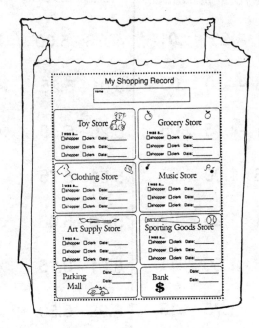

Store Signs

Each child also needs a sign containing their name to post when they are the manager/clerk of a store. The signs are slipped into a paper clip or through slits cut into the center's store sign.

Materials:
- marking pens or crayons
- 3" X 5" (7.5 X 13 cm) file cards

Steps:
1. Children print their names in large letters in pencil in their best handwriting on their file cards.

2. They trace the letters with marking pen or crayon.

Children keep the sign in their shopping bags when not in use.
You need to plan a safe place to store the shopping bags between center times.

Note: Reproduce this form to glue to shopping bags.

My Shopping Record

name

Toy Store

I was a...
☐ shopper ☐ clerk Date:_____

☐ shopper ☐ clerk Date:_____

☐ shopper ☐ clerk Date:_____

Grocery Store

I was a...
☐ shopper ☐ clerk Date:_____

☐ shopper ☐ clerk Date:_____

☐ shopper ☐ clerk Date:_____

Clothing Store

I was a...
☐ shopper ☐ clerk Date:_____

☐ shopper ☐ clerk Date:_____

☐ shopper ☐ clerk Date:_____

Music Store

I was a...
☐ shopper ☐ clerk Date:_____

☐ shopper ☐ clerk Date:_____

☐ shopper ☐ clerk Date:_____

Art Supply Store

I was a...
☐ shopper ☐ clerk Date:_____

☐ shopper ☐ clerk Date:_____

☐ shopper ☐ clerk Date:_____

Sporting Goods Store

I was a...
☐ shopper ☐ clerk Date:_____

☐ shopper ☐ clerk Date:_____

☐ shopper ☐ clerk Date:_____

Parking Mall

Date:_____

Date:_____

Bank $

Date:_____

Date:_____

Buying and Selling

Model

The teacher needs to model how each activity within the center is to be done. This includes showing what the customer will do and what the clerk will do. This is the point at which the teacher needs to explain what money can be used, whether change is made, and how to fill out any forms in the transaction.

Walk Through

After the teacher has modeled the process, students are chosen to walk through the steps as the teacher narrates what is to be done. Repeat this step until students are sure of what they are to do.

This is the point where you can also act out how to handle differences of opinion over the total cost of items and errors in making change.

Shopping "Etiquette"

Discuss and act out good shopping manners. Ask children to come up with a list of rules for being a polite shopper. Post these rules in class near the classroom shopping mall.

Cartoon Helpers

Show the cartoons from page 13. Explain how this works as a reminder of what to do when you are the buyer and when you are the seller.

Mall Rules
Walk in the centers.
Talk quietly.
Take your turn.
Wait in line.
Solve problems together.
Put things away when you are done.

Math at the Mall

The Shopper and the Clerk

Reproduce and use as a sign for this store in your classroom mall.

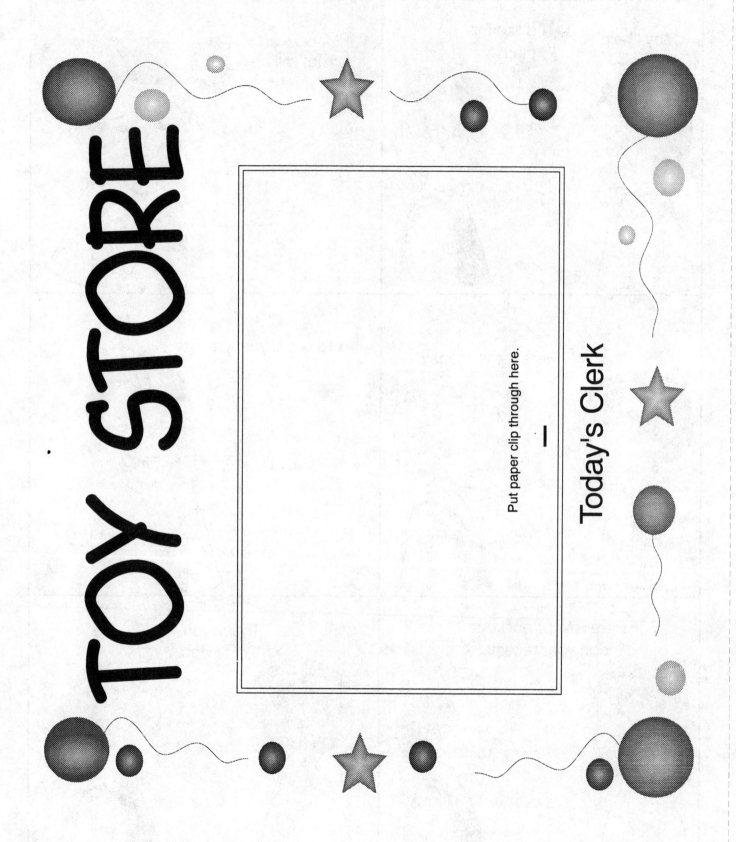

TOY STORE

Put paper clip through here.

Today's Clerk

Math Skills: recognizing and using money in the form of bills, counting out exact sums of money for payment and as change

Payment
Payment must be in exact amounts using paper bills. No change is given. The coin purse and cash box should contain only bills.

Preparations
Follow the general directions for setting up a store (see page 2).

- Price tags on toys should be in even dollar amounts.
- Provide a box labeled "Toys for Tots" where children can return toys.
- Prepare a set of cards (see pages 16 - 18 if they are going to be used.

Children may simply play with the toys they purchased or you may provide copies of the task cards on the following pages for extending the math challenges.

Procedures
Review what is to be done in the center by the shopper and by the clerk (see page 3).

Shopper
The shopper selects items to buy, being careful not to go over the amount in the coin purse. He/She adds up the total of the items selected, counts out the money needed for payment and takes the toys to the check-out stand. He/She gives the toys to the clerk and pays the requested amount. The shopper then returns to his/her desk and plays with the toys or does the activity on the task card.

Clerk
The clerk adds up the cost of the items purchased and accepts money. The items are put into the shopper's bag.

Toy Store

task 1

You can spend only [   ] .

Find the best buy you can make.

What did you buy? _____

_____

_____

_____

Draw a picture on the back to show how you play with it.

Toy Store

task 2

You are going to a birthday party.
The party is for twins.
You must buy two gifts that cost the same.

Draw the toys here.

Toy Store

task 3

Buy five toys.
List the toys and how much they cost.
Put them in order from the most to the least cost.

	toy	cost
1.		
2.		
3.		
4.		
5.		

Toy Store

task 4

Buy two toys.
Take the toys to your desk.
Look at the toys.
Keep the one you like best to play with.
Take the other toy back to the store.

How much money did you get back?

Draw the toys here.

I kept this toy.	I took this toy back.

Toy Store

task 5

Buy a toy you can build things with.
Take it to your desk.
Build something with the toy.

I built a _____.

It looked like this.

Toy Store

task 6

Buy these toys.
1. A toy with wheels
2. A toy that needs two children to play with it
3. A toy that looks like a person

Which toy cost the most money? _____

How much did it cost? _____

Which toy cost the least money? _____

How much did it cost? _____

What is the difference in
the cost of the two toys? _____

Reproduce and use as a sign for this store in your classroom mall.

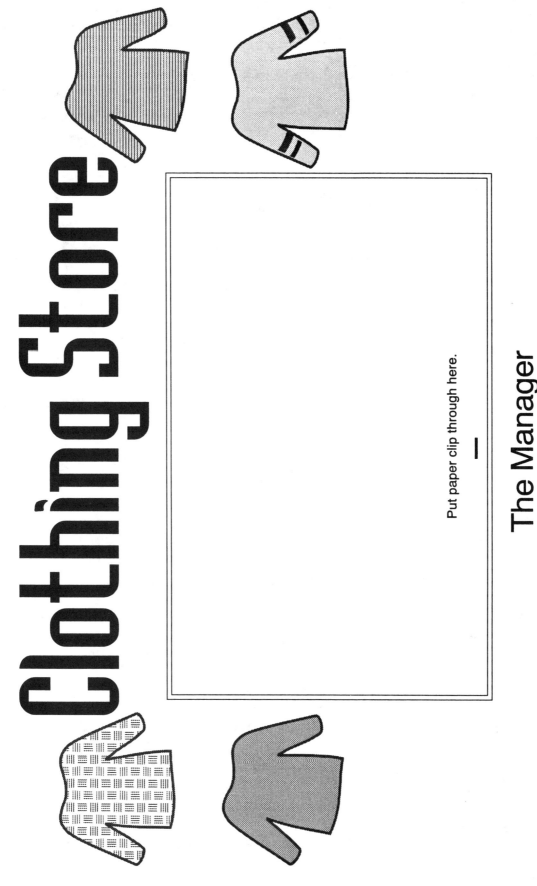

Clothing Store

Put paper clip through here.

The Manager

Math Skills: recognize and figure sums of money using bills, calculating change; filling out forms involving sums of money

Payment
Payment is in bills, but change can be made. Coin purses and the cash box should contain only bills.

Preparation
Follow the basic directions for setting up a center (see page 2). There are many types of clothing you can "sell" in this store. Both everyday clothing and "dress-up" clothes should be available.

- Price tags should contain only dollar amounts.
- Put the tagged items on a table or hang them from hangers on a laundry rack or in the coat closet.
- Set up a "charity box" where children can return items.
- Include a set of receipt slips (see page 8) and pencils.
- Prepare a set of task cards (see pages 21-23) if they are going to be used.
- Post the Shopper and Buyer cartoon.

Procedures
Review what is to be done in the center by the shopper and by the clerk (see page 3).

Shopper
In this store the shopper will receive a receipt from the clerk. The shopper checks the total on the receipt and pays the clerk. He/She checks to be sure the change is correct, then returns to his/her desk with the clothing. The shopper dresses up in the clothing and, if task cards are being done, completes the activity listed. When he/she is ready to purchase different clothing and/or has finished the task card, the clothes are placed in the "charity box" and a new purchase is made.

Clerk/Manager
The clerk will have to fill out a receipt form before asking for the payment. Change may need to be made.

Clothing Store — task 1

You are going to a costume party.
Buy what you need.

What did you buy?	How much did it cost?
_____	_____
_____	_____
_____	_____

How much did you spend in all? _____

Draw yourself dressed for the costume party.

Clothing Store — task 2

Buy a belt.
Use the belt to measure these:

1. How many belts long is your desk? _____

2. How many belts tall are you? _____
   Find a friend to help measure you.

3. How many belts wide is the classroom? _____

Draw the belt you used here.

Clothing Store task 3

You must buy a hat.
It is your story-telling hat.
Draw the hat here.

Wear the hat as you think up a story about the hat.
Tell the story to two friends.

What is the name of your story? _____

Did the hat help you make up a good story? _____

- -

Clothing Store task 4

You can only spend _____.
Look at what is for sale.
Think about the best buy you can make.

What did you buy? _____

_____

_____

_____

How much did you spend? _____

Did you get any change? _____ How much? _____

Clothing Store
task 5

You are going to buy a gift for someone in your family.
Think about what the gift is for.
Think about who the gift is for.

What did you buy? _____

_____

_____

Why did you pick this gift? _____

_____

_____

Draw the person opening the gift.

Clothing Store
task 6

You must buy three items that go together.

What did you buy?   What did it cost?

1. _____   _____

2. _____   _____

3. _____   _____

How much did you spend in all? _____

Draw the items. Show how they go together.

Reproduce and use as a sign for this store in your classroom mall.

Put paper clip through here.

Today's Clerk

Payment
Payment can be in coins and bills. Change can be made.

Preparations
Follow the basic directions for setting up a center (see page 2). There are many items you can "sell" in the music store. Some will depend on how much noise you can have in your classroom and if you have listening areas with headsets and tape or record players.
- Price tags should contain amount requiring coins or coins and bills as payment.
- Set up a "return box" where items may be placed at the end of center time. If you are using real tapes and records, have a special box for breakables and another box for musical instruments.
- Prepare a set of receipt forms containing a tax line (see page 8).
- Post a tax table (see page 9) and the buyer/seller cartoons in the center.
- Prepare a set of task cards (see pages 26 - 28) if they are going to be used.

Procedures
Review what is to be done in the center by the shopper and by the clerk (see page 3). Go over the shopper and clerk cartoon.

Shopper
In this center a tax is included in the price of the items. The shopper needs to check the receipt form to see if the total is correct, then pay for the purchase. The shopper returns to his/her desk or designated "music" area to listen to the tape or record, play with the instrument, or do the assigned task card.

Clerk
The clerk must calculate a subtotal on the receipt form, check the tax table, and make a final total. Change may need to be made.

Music Store — task 1

Buy a music tape or record.
Listen to the music.

What is the name of the tape or record? _____

_____

How much did it cost? _____

Did you like the music? _____ Why? _____

_____

_____

_____

_____

Music Store — task 2

Buy something you can use to make your own music.

Make up a song.
Play it for a friend.

Make a picture that shows you making music.

Music Store task 3

Buy a story tape or record.

Listen to the story.

What is the name of the story? _____

_____

Draw a picture of the part of the story you like best.

Music Store task 4

Buy a music tape or record.
Buy an instrument.

The tape or record cost_____ .

The instrument cost_____ .

I spent _____ in all.

Play along with the music with your instrument.

Music Store
task 5

You can spend _____ .
Look at what you can buy in the Music Store.
Make your best buy for this amount of money.

What did you buy? _____

How much did it cost? _____

Draw your "best buy" here.

Music Store
task 6

Buy five items.
Take them to your desk.

List the items in ABC order.
Tell what each one cost.

1. _____

2. _____

3. _____

4. _____

5. _____

I spent _____ in all.

Reproduce and use as a sign for this store in your classroom mall.

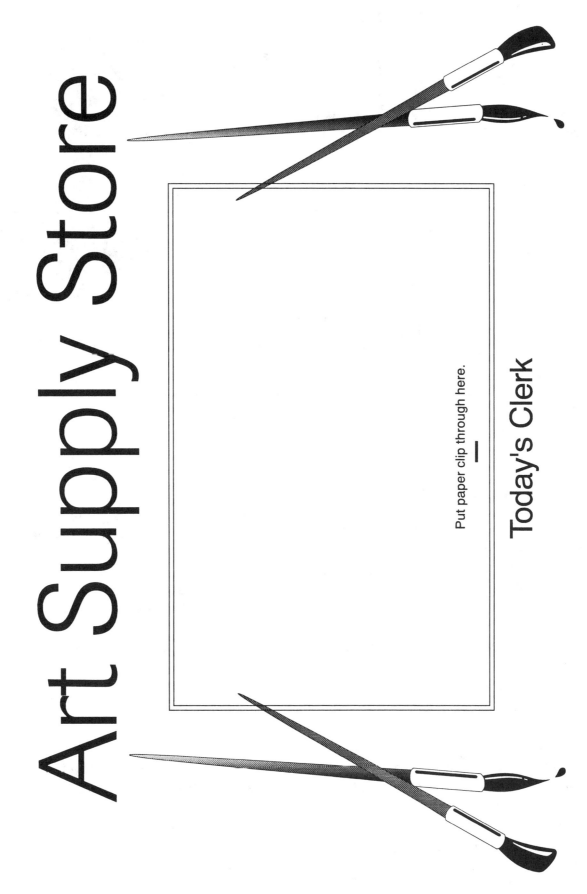

Art Supply Store

Put paper clip through here.

Today's Clerk

Math Skills: recognizing coins and their value, adding to find the total price, making change, filling in forms involving money

You might include:

clay

colored pencils

stamps

stamp pads

marking pens

special papers

glue sticks

blank "cards"

drawing paper

stars, stickers,

Payment

Payment can only be in coins. Change can be given.

Preparations

Follow the basic directions for setting up a center (see page 2). There are many items around the classroom that can be "sold" in this store. You will want to include high-interest items as well as a few special items. These will be used by the children, so review procedures for proper care.

- You may want to use only price tags containing amounts of no more than a dollar as children are practicing using only coins.
- Place a "recycle box" in the center for the return of materials.
- Include receipts with no tax line (see page 8).
- Prepare a set of task cards (see pages 31 - 33) if they are going to be used.

Procedures

Review what is to be done in the center by the shopper and by the clerk (see page 3).

Shopper

When all items have been paid for and the receipt form and change checked, the shopper returns to his/her desk and using the art materials completes the task card.

Clerk

The clerk adds up the cost of the items purchased, fills out the receipt form, accepts money, and gives any needed change. The items are put into the shopper's bag.

Art Store

task 1

You are a painter.
Buy what you need to paint a picture.

What did you buy?   How much did it cost?

_____   _____

_____   _____

_____   _____

How much did you spend in all? _____

Paint a picture.
Clean up your painting tools.
Return what you did not use to the Art Store.

Art Store

task 2

You are a sculptor.
Buy what you need to make an animal.

What did you buy?   How much did it cost?

_____   _____

_____   _____

_____   _____

How much did you spend in all? _____

Make an animal.
Return what you did not use to the Art Store.

Art Store
task 3

You are a printer.
Buy what you need to print a pattern.

What did you buy?	What did it cost?
_____	_____
_____	_____
_____	_____
_____	_____

How much did you spend in all? _____

Plan a pattern.
Show part of your pattern on the back of this card.

Return what you did not use to the Art Store.

Art Store
task 4

A special day is coming soon.
You need a greeting card.
Buy what you will need to make your card.

What did you buy?	What did it cost?
_____	_____
_____	_____
_____	_____
_____	_____

How much did you spend in all? _____
Make your card.
Who is the card for? _____

What special day is the card for? _____
Return what you did not use to the Art Store.

Art Store

task 5

You can spend _____ .
Think about what you want to make.
Make the best buys you can for this amount.
Can you get everything you need? _____

Draw a picture of what you made.

Art Store

task 6

Buy your favorite colors of crayons.
Make a picture with them.

How many crayons did you use? _____

How much did one cost? _____

How much did you spend on crayons in all? _____

Think about this:

If a box of eight crayons costs _____ ,

how much does one crayon cost? _____

Reproduce and use as a sign for this store in your classroom mall.

Sporting Goods Store

Put paper clip through here.

Today's Clerk

Math at the Mall

Payment

Payment can be in coins and bills. Change can be made.

Preparations: Follow the basic directions for setting up a center (see page 2). Set up a "play area" in class (or outside if you have supervision help) where children can use the sports equipment they "buy." You may need to stretch the definition of sport's equipment if the children have to remain in the classroom.

- Price tags can be in any amount appropriate for your students.
- Post a tax table (see page 9).
- Set a "recycle" box near the clerk's table.
- Include a copy of the buyer and seller cartoon as a student reminder.
- Prepare a set of task cards)see pages 36 - 38) if they are going to be used.

Procedures

Review what is to be done in the center by the shopper and by the clerk (see page 3).

Shopper

In this center, the shopper needs to figure out the actual cost of the items he/she wants to buy, then figure out the total including the tax. After paying, the shopper goes to the designated playing area to use the equipment or to his/her desk to complete the task card.

Clerk

The clerk must fill in the receipt form, adding up that amount, then adding on taxes to get the final total.

Sporting Goods task 1

Buy three items.
Take them to your desk.
Try out each one.

Draw a picture of the item that is the most fun.

Why do you like this best? _____

_____

Sporting Goods task 2

Buy two kinds of balls.
Draw the balls here.

Try the balls to see:

1. Which ball do you think will bounce the highest? _____

_____

Which ball did bounce the highest? _____

2. Which ball do you think you can roll the farthest? _____

_____

Which ball did roll the farthest? _____

Sporting Goods task 3

You must buy five items, but you can spend only _____.

What did you buy?	How much did it cost?
1. _____	_____
2. _____	_____
3. _____	_____
4. _____	_____
5. _____	_____

How much did you spend in all?_____

How much money did you have left?_____

Sporting Goods task 4

Buy a jump rope.
Find an open space where you can jump.

See how many times you can do these.

1. How many times can you jump without missing?

_____

2. How many times can you jump doing "hot pepper"?

_____

3. How high can you count by _____s before you miss?

_____

Sporting Goods — task 5

Buy five sports cards.
Take them to your desk.

List the names of the players in ABC order.

1. _____

2. _____

3. _____

4. _____

5. _____

How much did you spend in all? _____

How much did one card cost? _____

Sporting Goods — task 6

You have three friends coming over after school.
Buy two things you can all play with together.

What did you buy?   What did it cost?

1. _____

2. _____

Which one cost the most? _____

How much more did it cost than the other one? _____

Reproduce and use as a sign for this store in your classroom mall.

Grocery Store

Put paper clip through here.

Today's Clerk

Math Skills: column addition, recognizing the value of various forms of money, subtraction, filling in a form using money symbols

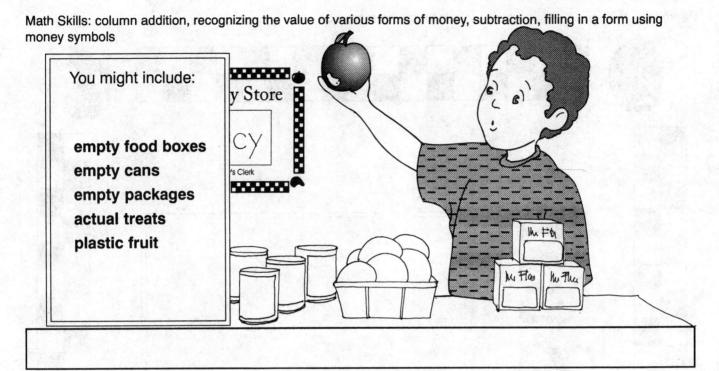

Payment

Payment may be made in coins and bills. Change can be given.

Preparation

See page 49 for a parent letter requesting that small, clean, empty food containers be sent to school. You may want to limit the variety that is for sale at any one time.

• Put copies of the coupons from page 41 on the table. Shoppers may help themselves as they make their selection. You can vary the value of the coupons to match your students' math level.
• Post a copy of the tax table (see page 9).
• Include a set of receipt slips and pencils.
• Set up a set of "recycle" boxes (paper, cans, cardboard) near the clerk's table.
• Provide a calculator and pencil for the clerk.
• Prepare a set of task cards (see pages 42 - 44) if they are to be used.

Procedure

Review what is to be done in the center by the shopper and by the clerk (see page 3).

Shopper

The shopper selects items to buy. He/She can use any appropriate coupons from the supply on the table. The shopper gives the items being purchased to the clerk. The shopper pays the correct amount, and takes the items and task card to his/her desk.

Clerk

The clerk calculates the coupon discounts and fills in the receipt. He/She adds the tax to the subtotal and checks the total on the calculator. The clerk takes the payment and gives the correct change.

                                                                               Math at the Mall

Coupon

25 cents off

1/2 off

Coupon

Coupon

10 CENTS OFF

Coupon

1/4 off

50 cents off

Coupon

Coupon

Buy 2
Get 1 FREE

Coupon

Save 30 cents

2 for the price of one

Coupon

Math at the Mall

Grocery Store task 1

Think of three things you want to buy.
See if you can find coupons for them.

I bought:	It cost:	Coupon (yes or no):	I saved:
1. _____	_____	_____	_____
2. _____	_____	_____	_____
3. _____	_____	_____	_____

I spent _____ for the three things.

- -

Grocery Store task 2

You are going on a picnic with a friend.

Make a list of what you got for the picnic.
Tell how much you spent for the food.

I bought:	I spent:
_____	_____
_____	_____
_____	_____
_____	_____
_____	_____

Draw yourself and your friend at the picnic.

Grocery Store task 3

You must buy a cereal and soup.
Find the best buy you can make.
See if you can find coupons to help you save.

I bought: It cost:

_____ cereal   _____

_____ soup   _____

This is how much I saved: _____

_____

Grocery Store task 4

Buy five items
Use coupons if you can.
Take them to your desk.
List the items in order.
Start with the one that cost the most.
End with the one that cost the least.

I bought: It cost:

1. _____   _____

2. _____   _____

3. _____   _____

4. _____   _____

5. _____   _____

Grocery Store task 5

Grocery Store
Buy something for lunch.
You can spend only _____ .

Draw what you got.
Put the cost by the items.

How much did you spend in all?

_____

Grocery Store task 6

Buy three kinds of fruit.
What did you buy?   What did it cost?

1. _____ _____

2. _____ _____

3. _____ _____

How much did you spend in all? _____

Draw the fruit that cost the most here.

Draw the fruit that cost the least here.

Other Stores You May Have in Your Mall

You don't need to stop at the stores in this book. Create others of your own. Here are some you might choose.

Shoe Store

Include all types of shoes, boots, slippers, sandals plus a "shoe size" guide, a chair for the customer, and a low stool for the clerk.

Book Store

Include fiction, nonfiction, and student-authored books plus magazines and newspapers.

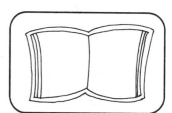

Card Shop

Provide blank cards and envelopes for children to decorate and "cards" run on colored paper stating traditional greetings such as "Happy Birthday," "Congratulations," etc., which children can purchase to send to friends and family members.

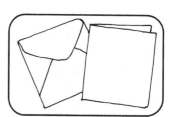

Restaurant

Set up a table with a tablecloth, flowers, and dishes. Provide a menu of food which can be ordered from your restaurant. This can be imaginary taste treats or you can go all out and have items such as peanut butter sandwiches which can be eaten. You will need a waitperson and a cook.

Now that you have this busy mall, you may want to add a parking garage in which all those busy shoppers may park their cars. This is a good way to add the element of telling time to your math activities. You will find directions for a parking garage on page 47.

Math at the Mall

Reproduce this and use as a sign in your classroom mall.

PARKING GARAGE

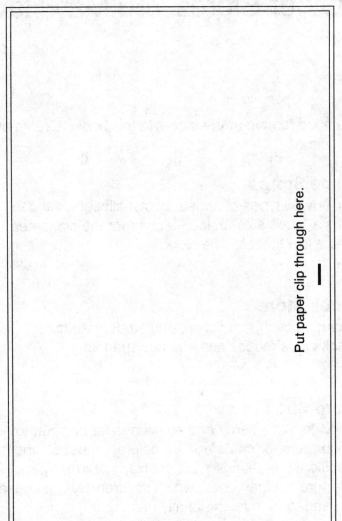

Please take a time ticket.

Bring your ticket back with you when you are done.

Put paper clip through here.

Today's Parking Attendant

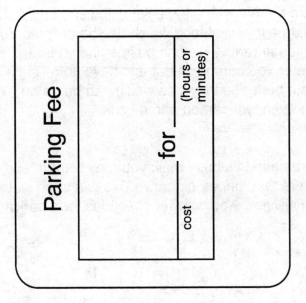

Parking Fee

_____ for _____
cost   (hours or minutes)

46

Math at the Mall

Parking Garage

PARKING GARAGE
Please take a time ticket.
Bring your ticket back with you when you are done.

Parking Fee

_____ for _____
(hours or minutes)

Sam

Put paper slip through here

Today's Parking Attendant

This activity can be used most effectively when students are doing independent activities where the length of time they spend varies. It will also be particularly effective when you combine the activities in this book for a "Mall Day."

Use a table for your parking garage. The table needs to be within view of the classroom clock. Students enjoy parking toy cars in this activity.

When the shopper arrives at the mall to park a car, the attendant writes the time on a ticket and gives it to the customer. When the shopper returns to claim his vehicle, the current time is written on the ticket. The charge is calculated based on the rate posted. You can vary the rate to make the math more or less difficult.

Parking
Ticket

	for each	hour 1/2 hour 10 min.

Time in: _____ : _____

Time out: _____ : _____

Time parked _____ : _____

Parking Fee

Extension Activities

After your students have sampled the *Math at the Mall* activities, provide real-life experiences of the same type.

Field Trips
If you have the ability to take field trips to stores in town, it can provide a valuable connection of classroom learning to the real world. Discuss what to look for before the trip. It helps to have simple worksheets for students to use on the trip. Include checklists of things to look for and questions to be answered by observation or interview.

Guest Speakers
If you have local merchants come in, be sure to explain what it is you want them to emphasize. Ask them to bring along examples of the forms they use, etc.

Business Activities at School
There are practical examples that can be shared with your students right on your school campus. Take a "behind the scenes" tour of your school cafeteria. Have the manager explain how food is ordered and paid for. Ask the school secretary to explain about purchase orders and billing for school supplies. How about the custodial supplies? Explain the economics of bake sales and book faires.

Classroom Economy
A natural next-step for the activities in this book would be to set up a simple economy for your classroom using play money. Students can earn money for classwork or homework and buy privileges or simple prizes. This simple start can be expanded into more complex economies with banks and businesses, depending on the sophistication of your group.

Parent Involvement
The letter on the inside-back cover encourages your parents to include their children in shopping experiences and to share how they use checks, credit cards, etc.

48